Beyond the Page

A Guide to Marketing for Authors

Richard Fierce

Dragonfire Press

Copyright © 2024 by Richard Fierce

All rights reserved.

No portion of this book may be reproduced in any form without written permission from the publisher or author, except as permitted by U.S. copyright law.

Contents

1. Who Am I?   1
2. Mindset   5
3. Paid Newsletters   12
4. Amazon Ads   17
5. How to Create an Amazon Ad   24
6. Facebook Ads   30
7. How to Create a Facebook Ad   36
8. In Person Events   42
9. The Art of the Blurb   63
10. Paid Newsletter Resources   73

About the author   78

Chapter 1

Who Am I?

I'm sure you're wondering that, right? Who is this guy, and why does he think he can speak on marketing? I'm so glad you asked! Before I tell you who I am, let me tell you who I am **not**.

I'm not a marketing guru. I don't claim to have some magic bullet for marketing books that if you follow steps X, Y, and Z, you're guaranteed to sell books. I hate to break it to you, but if that's what you're looking for, you will never find it. There is no magic bullet. I think that bears repeating.

There is no magic bullet.

That doesn't mean that nothing works. It's quite the opposite, actually. But I'm getting ahead of myself. This guide isn't to tell you what you should do, but instead, it's going to tell you what I do *that works for me*. This is an important thing to note because what works for one author won't necessarily work for another. And I had to learn that the hard way, many times over.

So, who am I? I'm an author who writes primarily young adult (YA) fantasy. On top of that, I write short books, most of which fall between 20-30,000 words in length. This word count is known as novella length. I write these novellas in episodic format as series. My longest series (at the time of writing this) is 15 books. This is another important thing to note because series is where the money is.

Now, if you're a hobby author and aren't looking to make a profit on your work, there's absolutely nothing wrong with that. The tips in this book can help you as well, but this book is more aimed at those who want to make money from their work.

I've been self-publishing since 2007, which is basically when the Kindle came out. I've made so many mistakes I can't even list them all. I tell you that so you know I'm speaking from experience.

Since 2020, I've sold over 200,000 copies of my books across all formats (ebook, audio, and print). I'm not a million selling author (yet), but that's also nothing to balk at considering the average self-published book (digital only) sells 250 copies in its lifetime. By comparison, traditionally published books average 3,000 copies.

Now that you know a little about me, let's get into what you're really reading this book for.

Chapter 2

Mindset

There are a few things you'll need to decide before you start marketing your books, and most of them deal with your mindset. You need to ask yourself a few questions, such as:

What is my ultimate goal?

Is writing books a business for me, or a hobby?

There are others, but let's focus on these because they will help determine your mindset about marketing. If your ultimate goal is to just get your book into the hands of readers and you don't care about making a profit, then you likely don't care if you lose money on marketing. And that's completely fine.

However, if you view publishing your books as a business, you don't want to lose money. You want to make it. Not literally, of course, because that's illegal. See what I did there? Every marketing tactic you implement should be driven by your ultimate goal. For authors like me, it's to make money on your books.

While writing may begin as a passion or a hobby for most of us, self-publishing transforms it into a viable entrepreneurial venture. Here's why authors should adopt a business mindset when it comes to self-publishing:

Professionalism Breeds Success: Treating your writing endeavors as a business demands a commitment to professionalism in every aspect of your work. From editing to cover design, marketing, and distribution, approaching each task with a business mindset ensures a high standard of quality that resonates with readers.

Understanding Market Demand: In business, success hinges on meeting market demand. Similarly, authors must conduct market research to understand reader preferences, trends, and gaps in the literary landscape. This insight informs content creation, helping authors tailor their work to meet the needs and expectations of their target audience.

Strategic Planning and Goal Setting: A business mindset encourages authors to set clear, achievable goals and develop strategic plans to reach them. Whether it's outlining a series of books, setting sales targets, or expanding into new genres, strategic planning lays the foundation for long-term success in self-publishing.

Financial Sustainability: Viewing self-publishing as a business underscores the importance of financial sustainability. Authors must consider revenue streams, pricing strategies, and investment in marketing and promotion to ensure profitability. By managing finances effectively, authors can reinvest profits into their writing career, fueling growth and expansion.

Building a Brand: Successful businesses are built on strong brands that resonate with their target audience. Authors must cultivate their author brand, encompassing their writing style, genre specialization, and unique voice. Consistent branding across platforms and marketing efforts fosters reader loyalty and distinguishes authors in a crowded marketplace.

Embracing Entrepreneurial Spirit: At its core, self-publishing embodies the spirit of entrepreneurship. Authors navigate the challenges of self-promotion, distribution, and competition, taking ownership of their creative destiny. Embracing this entrepreneurial spirit empowers authors to adapt to market changes, seize opportunities, and innovate within the publishing industry.

Maximizing Efficiency: Time is a valuable resource for any business, and self-publishing is no exception. Adopting a business mindset encourages authors to streamline their workflow, leverage technology, and outsource tasks when necessary. By maximizing efficiency, authors can focus more time and energy on writing and growing their business.

Networking and Collaboration: Business thrives on networking and collaboration, and the same holds true for self-publishing. Authors benefit from connecting with fellow writers, industry professionals, and readers through online communities, social media, and literary events. These connections facilitate knowledge sharing, support, and potential partnerships that enhance the author's publishing journey.

The transition from viewing self-publishing as a hobby to treating it as a business is essential for authors aspiring to thrive in the competitive world of independent publishing.

By embracing professionalism, strategic thinking, financial acumen, and entrepreneurial spirit, authors can unlock their full potential and build sustainable careers as self-published authors. So, let's shift our mindset, and embark on this journey with the determination and vision of successful entrepreneurs.

Chapter 3

Paid Newsletters

In today's rapidly evolving landscape of self-publishing, finding effective marketing strategies is paramount to standing out in the crowd. With countless books vying for readers' attention, indie authors face the challenge of not only producing compelling stories but also ensuring it reaches the right audience. One strategy that has gained significant traction is leveraging paid newsletters.

So, what is a paid newsletter? Paid newsletters are email lists, usually divided by genre, where you can pay to include your book on a specific date. These newsletters offer a unique opportunity to reach potential readers who have an interest in specific genres or niches. There are so many of these services available, you can literally book a slot in a newsletter every week for the entire year -and I do just that!

The ROI (return on investment) of these newsletters ranges all over the board, and you will find some perform better for you than others. The benefits of using paid newsletters are many, including:

Targeted Reach: Paid newsletters cater to specific audiences in particular topics or genres. By placing your book in the correct category, you can ensure your promotional efforts reach readers who are more likely to be interested in your work. This approach increases the chances of a potential reader connecting with your book.

Establishing Authority: Collaborating with reputable newsletter services allows authors to leverage the credibility of these platforms. When featured in a curated newsletter, authors gain validation from the newsletter's audience, positioning themselves as trusted voices within their niche. This can be instrumental in building a loyal readership base.

Driving Sales: Promoting books through paid newsletters can lead to tangible results in terms of sales and engagement. With dedicated sections highlighting recommended reads or exclusive discounts, authors can incentivize readers to purchase their books. By continuously using these services, authors can maintain momentum and sustain interest in their work over time.

Measurable Impact: Unlike some other marketing tactics where gauging effectiveness can be challenging, paid newsletters offer authors a way to see tangible results. Booking promotions at least a week apart helps to identify which platforms are reaching the readers you're looking for. This data-driven approach will enable you to make informed decisions about where to allocate your dollars for maximum impact.

It should go without saying that you must write a good book. It needs to be edited. You need to have a professional book cover. Your blurb must be enticing. All of these things are key to ensuring that when you do market your books, readers don't hesitate to buy them. I have included a list of paid newsletters you can use to promote your books with in the next section.

Chapter 4

Amazon Ads

In today's digital age, where the competition for readers' attention is fiercer than ever, authors need to leverage every available tool to promote their books effectively. Among the plethora of marketing options, Amazon Ads stand out as a powerful tool for reaching potential readers directly on the world's largest online marketplace. Whether you're a seasoned author or just starting out, understanding how to harness the potential of Amazon Ads can significantly boost your book sales and visibility.

Understanding Amazon Ads

Amazon Ads are a form of pay-per-click (PPC) advertising that allows authors to promote their books within Amazon's ecosystem. These ads appear in various locations on Amazon, including search results, product pages, and even on Kindle e-readers. The key advantage of Amazon Ads is their ability to target potential readers based on their search queries and browsing behavior, making them highly relevant and impactful.

Setting Up Your Amazon Ads Campaign

Define your goals: Before launching an ad campaign, it's essential to clearly define your objectives. Whether you aim to increase book sales or boost visibility, having specific goals will help you tailor your campaign accordingly.

Keyword Research: Keywords play a crucial role in ensuring your ads reach the right audience. Conduct thorough keyword research to identify relevant terms and phrases that potential readers are likely to use when searching for books similar to yours. Tools like Publisher Rocket can assist you in this process. If you're on a limited budget, you can open a browser window in Incognito Mode and type in keywords you're thinking of using. If it populates as an option, it means there are people searching for that word or phrase. If not, don't use it.

Create Compelling Ad Copy: Craft engaging ad copy that highlights the unique selling points of your book. Focus on captivating headlines and concise yet compelling descriptions that entice readers to click through to your product page.

Set Your Budget and Bidding Strategy: Determine your daily budget and bidding strategy based on your advertising goals and budget constraints. Amazon offers two main bidding options: automatic and manual. Automatic targeting allows Amazon to optimize your ad placements based on its algorithms, while manual targeting gives you more control over which keywords to bid on.

Have an Eye-Catching Book Cover: Visual appeal is key to grabbing readers' attention amidst the sea of competing books. Invest in high-quality book covers that stand out and accurately represent your book's content. A lot of authors struggle in this area. The worst thing you can do is make your own cover to save money. Your book cover is the first thing that a reader sees. If it looks DIY, readers will pass on it. If you can only invest in one thing, it should be your cover.

Optimizing Your Amazon Ads Campaign

Monitor Performance Metrics: Keep a close eye on key performance metrics such as click-through rate (CTR), conversion rate, and cost per click (CPC). Analyzing these metrics will help you identify what's working well and where optimizations are needed.

Refine Targeting and Keywords: Continuously refine your targeting parameters and keyword selection based on performance data. Experiment with different keyword match types (broad, phrase, exact) and adjust bids to maximize your ad's effectiveness.

A/B Testing: Test different headlines and calls-to-action to determine which combinations yield the best results. Split testing allows you to identify which elements resonate most with your target audience and optimize accordingly.

Optimize Product Pages: Ensure that your book's product page is optimized for conversions by providing a compelling blurb. A well-optimized product page can significantly impact the effectiveness of your ad campaigns.

Scale Successful Campaigns: Once you've identified high-performing keywords and ad copy, consider scaling up your campaigns by increasing your budget or expanding your targeting parameters. However, always monitor performance closely to ensure continued success.

Amazon Ads offer authors a powerful platform to promote their books directly to a highly targeted audience of potential readers. By understanding the fundamentals of Amazon advertising and implementing effective strategies for campaign setup, optimization, and refinement, authors can significantly enhance their book sales and visibility in the competitive online marketplace. Remember, success with Amazon Ads requires ongoing experimentation, analysis, and adaptation to stay ahead of the curve in the ever-evolving world of book marketing.

Chapter 5

How to Create an Amazon Ad

Navigating the intricacies of Amazon Ads can be daunting for authors new to the platform. Fear not! In this step-by-step guide, I'll walk you through the process of creating an Amazon Ad to promote your book.

Step 1: Navigate to Amazon Advertising

Log in to your Amazon Author Central account. If you don't have one, you can easily create one.

Once logged in, navigate to the "Marketing" tab and select "Amazon Advertising."

Step 2: Choose Your Campaign Type

Click on "Create Campaign" and select the campaign type. For promoting books, the most suitable option is typically "Sponsored Products."

Step 3: Set Your Campaign Details

Give your campaign a name that is easy to identify and remember.

Decide on your daily budget. Start with a modest amount, and you can always adjust it later based on performance.

Choose the duration of your campaign. You can either set a specific end date or run it continuously.

Step 4: Select Targeting Options

Determine your target audience based on relevant keywords, interests, or specific books or authors.

Choose the bidding strategy that aligns with your budget and advertising goals. Options include dynamic bids (down only), dynamic bids (up and down), and fixed bids. I recommend using fixed bids.

Step 5: Create Ad Groups

Divide your campaign into ad groups based on similar targeting or themes.

Set your default bid for each ad group. This bid represents the maximum amount you're willing to pay when a customer clicks on your ad.

Step 6: Create Your Ad

Write a compelling ad headline that grabs attention and accurately represents your book.

Craft concise ad copy that highlights the unique selling points of your book and encourages users to click.

Step 7: Review and Launch Your Campaign

Double-check all the details of your campaign, including budget, targeting, and ad content.

Once you're satisfied, click on "Launch Campaign" to set your ads live.

Step 8: Monitor and Optimize

Keep a close eye on the performance of your ads using Amazon Advertising's reporting tools.

Monitor key metrics such as click-through rate (CTR), conversion rate, and cost-per-click (CPC).

Make adjustments to your campaign as needed, such as tweaking keywords, adjusting bids, or refining targeting options.

Step 9: Iterate and Improve

Continuously analyze the data gathered from your campaigns to identify what's working and what isn't.

Experiment with different ad creatives, targeting strategies, and bidding techniques to optimize performance.

Don't be afraid to iterate and refine your approach based on the insights you gain from running multiple campaigns.

By following this step-by-step guide, you can create effective Amazon Ads that increase the visibility of your book and drive sales. Remember to stay vigilant, monitor your campaigns closely, and always be willing to adapt and refine your strategies to achieve the best results.

Chapter 6

Facebook Ads

Facebook, with its massive user base and advanced targeting capabilities, offers indie authors a unique platform to reach potential readers. With over 2.8 billion monthly active users, Facebook provides access to a diverse audience spanning different demographics, interests, and geographic locations. This vast reach allows authors to tailor their marketing efforts to specific segments of the population, ensuring that their ads resonate with the right audience.

Crafting Compelling Ad Campaigns

The key to success with Facebook Ads lies in crafting compelling and engaging campaigns that capture the attention of potential readers. You should invest time and effort into creating visually appealing ad creatives that showcase book covers, blurbs, and endorsements. High-quality images and concise, captivating copy are essential for grabbing attention amidst the clutter of the newsfeed.

Moreover, you can leverage Facebook's targeting options to narrow down their audience based on factors such as age, gender, location, interests, and reading habits. By refining your targeting parameters, you can ensure that your ads are shown to users who are most likely to be interested in your genre or niche.

Maximizing ROI through Data-Driven Strategies

One of the most significant advantages of Facebook Ads is the wealth of data and analytics available to advertisers. You can track the performance of your ad campaigns in real-time, monitoring metrics such as impressions, clicks, and conversions. By analyzing this data, you can gain valuable insights into the effectiveness of your ads and make informed decisions to optimize your campaigns for better results.

For instance, you can experiment with different ad formats, audience segments, and messaging to see which combinations yield the best results. A/B testing allows you to compare different variations of your ads and identify which elements resonate most with their target audience. By continuously refining your approach based on data-driven insights, you can maximize your return on investment (ROI) and achieve your marketing objectives more efficiently.

Building Relationships and Driving Engagement

Beyond just promoting your books, you can use Facebook Ads to build meaningful relationships with readers and foster engagement. By sharing behind-the-scenes content, author interviews, and exclusive sneak peeks, you can create a sense of intimacy and connection with your audience. Encouraging readers to interact with your ads through likes, comments, and shares can help increase organic reach and amplify the impact of your marketing efforts.

Furthermore, you can leverage Facebook's retargeting capabilities to re-engage users who have previously interacted with your content or visited your website. By serving targeted ads to this warm audience segment, you can nurture leads and guide them further down the sales funnel, ultimately increasing conversion rates and book sales.

Facebook Ads offer indie authors a powerful platform to promote their books, connect with their audience, and drive sales. By leveraging Facebook's extensive targeting options, crafting compelling ad campaigns, and analyzing data-driven insights, authors can maximize their marketing ROI and achieve their business objectives effectively. With strategic planning and creative execution, you can harness the full potential of Facebook Ads to elevate your author brand and reach new heights of success in the competitive world of publishing.

Chapter 7

How to Create a Facebook Ad

Facebook Ads can help authors amplify their book's visibility and attract potential readers. In this step-by-step guide, I'll walk you through the process of creating a Facebook Ad campaign to effectively advertise your book.

Step 1: Define Your Campaign Objective

Before diving into creating your Facebook Ad, it's crucial to clarify your campaign objective. Ask yourself, what do you want to achieve with this ad? Do you aim to increase book sales, drive traffic to your website, or raise awareness about your book? Select the appropriate campaign objective from Facebook's options, such as "Traffic," "Conversions," or "Engagement," based on your goal. For book sales, I recommend Traffic ads.

Step 2: Identify Your Target Audience

One of the key advantages of Facebook Ads is the ability to target specific demographics, interests, and behaviors. Define your target audience based on factors such as age, gender, location, interests, and book genres relevant to your book. Facebook provides robust targeting options, allowing you to tailor your ad to reach the most relevant audience likely to be interested in your book.

Step 3: Craft Compelling Ad Creative

Create attention-grabbing ad creative that effectively communicates the value proposition of your book. This includes selecting an eye-catching image or video that resonates with your target audience, along with compelling ad copy that highlights the key features and benefits of your book. Use concise and persuasive language to entice viewers to learn more or take action, such as "Shop Now" or "Download."

Step 4: Set Your Budget and Schedule

Determine your ad budget and schedule to ensure optimal allocation of resources. Facebook offers flexible budgeting options, allowing you to set a daily or lifetime budget for your campaign. Additionally, you can specify the duration of your ad campaign by selecting start and end dates or running it continuously. Experiment with different budget levels and scheduling options to find the most effective strategy for your book promotion.

Step 5: Choose Ad Placement

Facebook offers various ad placement options across its platform, including the News Feed, right column, Messenger, and Instagram. Select the ad placements that align with your campaign objectives and target audience preferences. For example, if your goal is to drive website traffic, consider placing your ad in the News Feed for maximum visibility and engagement.

Step 6: Monitor and Optimize Performance

Once your Facebook Ad campaign is live, monitor its performance closely using Facebook Ads Manager. Track key metrics such as reach, engagement, click-through rate (CTR), and conversion rate to evaluate the effectiveness of your ad. Analyze the data to identify any areas for improvement and make necessary adjustments to optimize your campaign for better results. Experiment with different ad creative, targeting options, and messaging to refine your approach and maximize the impact of your book promotion efforts. I recommend running an ad for at least 7 days to get enough data to make informed decisions.

Facebook Ads offer authors a powerful platform to reach their target audience and promote their books effectively. By following these step-by-step instructions and leveraging Facebook's advanced targeting and optimization features, you can create compelling ad campaigns that drive book sales, increase brand awareness, and engage with readers on a deeper level.

Chapter 8

In Person Events

In a world increasingly dominated by digital platforms and online sales, there's something undeniably special about connecting with readers face-to-face at in-person events. Whether it's a book fair, literary festival, or author signing, these events provide a unique opportunity for authors to engage directly with their audience and boost sales. However, making the most of these occasions requires careful planning and execution. Here are some invaluable tips and advice for authors looking to excel at in-person sales events.

Preparation is Key

Research the event thoroughly: Understand the demographics of attendees, the layout of the venue, and any rules or regulations set by the organizers.

Stock up on inventory: Ensure you have an ample supply of books, promotional materials, and any other merchandise you plan to sell. It's better to bring too many books than not enough.

Practice your pitch: Develop a concise and compelling elevator pitch that highlights the key selling points of your book. Don't get discouraged when people say 'no.' This will happen, and it's important to remember your book isn't for everyone. Art is subjective.

Create an Eye-Catching Display

Design an attractive booth or table setup that reflects the tone and themes of your book.

Utilize signage, banners, and decorations to draw attention to your display and make it stand out in a crowded venue.

Arrange your books and merchandise in an organized and visually appealing manner to encourage browsing and impulse purchases.

Engage with Attendees

Be approachable and friendly: Smile, make eye contact, and greet people as they pass by your booth.

Initiate conversations: Strike up conversations with attendees about your book, their reading preferences, or related topics to build rapport and establish a connection.

Offer personalized recommendations: If you don't have the type of book a reader is interested in, suggest other authors or books you know do match their interests.

Offer Incentives and Special Deals

Provide incentives to encourage sales, such as bundle deals, but remember not to cut yourself short.

Offer signed copies or personalized messages to add value and make your books more desirable to potential buyers.

Leverage Technology

Accept multiple forms of payment: Ensure you can process transactions quickly and conveniently by accepting cash, credit/debit cards, and mobile payments.

Use technology to capture leads: Collect email addresses or social media handles from interested attendees to follow up with them after the event.

Utilize social media and event hashtags to promote your presence at the event and attract attendees to your booth.

Follow Up After the Event

Send thank-you emails to attendees: Express your appreciation for their support and provide links to where they can purchase your book online if they didn't make a purchase at the event.

Continue the conversation: Engage with attendees on social media or through email to maintain the connection and nurture relationships beyond the event.

Request feedback: Ask attendees for their thoughts on your booth setup, presentation, and overall experience to gather valuable insights for future events.

Other Considerations

Don't feel like you have to do everything all at once. Begin with something small and local. Look for events in your immediate area, such as a farmer's market or community craft fair, and give it a try. Instead of diving into purchasing all the necessary equipment for multiple shows, it's wise to test the waters first.

Which types of books are successful at live events?

When it comes to genre, opportunities are abundant. Events centered around a specific theme such as comic cons, horror cons, or gaming cons tend to attract readers interested in those genres. However, conventional publishing advice suggests focusing on one genre and building a following there. In my personal experience with live events, I've found the opposite to be true. For live events, having a diverse range of genres available is actually a strength rather than a weakness.

What kinds of events should authors look for?

Where can you find your readers? What types of events would interest them? Romance enthusiasts are a diverse group, constantly seeking new books to delve into. According to Amazon, the top genres are romance, mystery/suspense/thriller, and sci-fi/fantasy. If you write in any of these popular genres, chances are you'll come across your readers at large events where people gather together. I have had great success connecting with fans of sci-fi, fantasy, romance, and crime thrillers at the following kinds of events:

Comic cons (both big ones and smaller local pop-up events)

Craft fairs (people who appreciate handmade crafts usually prefer printed books)

Themed events (horror conventions, anime conventions, sci-fi and fantasy conventions)

Mall events (people are already coming there to spend money)

Festivals (if lots of people attend, at least some of them are bound to be readers)

Gaming conventions (tabletop games take up a lot of trunk space, and so do books)

Notice that I didn't include book fairs on this list. I've done a handful of these, and they've been fine, but when you do a book fair, you're signing up to compete directly with every other author there. Sure, the audience is 100% readers, but I've personally found much more success in showing up to events where people aren't expecting to see an author there.

What costs should authors expect to budget for?

As with most publishing ventures, authors can expect to face a range of expenses with live events. If your long term goal is to do multiple events, you can gradually tackle some of these expenses over time. For each show you do, chances are good that you'll end up paying something for the space at the event. I've paid as little as $35 for a spot, and the most I've paid is $470-ish for a spot at a huge show (where it's possible to do over 10 times that much in revenue). You'll inevitably pay for gas and other travel-related expenses, possibly shipping expenses to get your books to the venue (though I'd recommend bringing them with you if possible), lodging for overnight shows, and food. When possible, I hit up local grocery stores and get stuff to make sandwiches to save money. Naturally, you'll have to buy the books themselves, too. Buying in bulk can save money, but make sure you have somewhere safe and dry to store them. Those are all pretty "normal" or "routine" recurring expenses for doing shows, but authors also need to account for less obvious expenses. Most of the following are one-time expenses, so once you have them, you're set (until they get lost or wear out, etc.):

Banners or signs – You'll want to have your backdrop and signs professionally designed and printed. Do it right the first time, and you won't have to replace it unless it gets damaged.

Banner stand – If you buy a banner, you've got to hang it on something. Don't count on the venue letting you tack it to their wall. Buy and bring your own setup instead.

Tables and tablecloths – Not all venues and events provide tables. Even if they do, you might need more table space than they offer, so buying and bringing your own tables is a good idea. Most events also require you to cover your tables so everything looks professional, so invest in some tablecloths.

Shelves and other display elements – If you have a lot of books, a good strategy to employ is to build UPWARD rather than outward. Maximize your vendor space by displaying books on bookshelves, both freestanding and tabletop versions.

Floor mats – If you're standing all day, your feet will pay the price. I recommend buying some padded floor mats to give your old dogs a break.

A comfortable chair – As with the floor mats, a good chair is useful when you need to take a minute to rest, or when you need to sit down to sign a book (or several). Bonus points if it has cupholders.

Signing implements – I recommend using a Sharpie, preferably in a unique color of your choice, to sign books. Sharpie ink doesn't fade, and you get to express your personality when you pick a cool color.

Something sharp – Scissors, a knife, a claymore — you might need a tool to cut something at some point.

Sales/credit card processing software – I use Square. They don't charge up front (except to buy one of their card readers, if you need one), but they do take a minimal percentage of each sale. Price your books accordingly so your margins don't suffer.

Cash stash – Avoid coins. Bring small bills (ones and fives), and round up or down as needed.

Bins for your books and supplies – You can certainly haul books in boxes, but I've found that using clear plastic bins is a great alternative because you can see exactly what's inside. Make sure you also have a container or a box to transport your "extras" from the list above. If it's all in one place, it's easier to ensure it won't get left behind.

A hefty cart – Trust me when I say you don't want to skimp on your cart. Get something you can manage in terms of your physical well-being; for me, that's a big multi-positional dolly.

As a reminder, you don't need to buy everything on this list right away. If you're planning to do a lot of events, then it's wise to invest in these things, but you can spread it out. My display setup came together one piece at a time, or occasionally two or three pieces at a time, as needed.

How can authors price their books to cover all of these expenses?

I've found success in pricing my individual books based on the 1/3-split metric. Essentially, the breakdown is as follows:

1/3 of your retail price covers the cost of printing the book

1/3 covers the cost to replace the copy of the book you just sold

1/3 is revenue or profit, to be applied to other expenses as necessary

So if your book costs $5.00 to print, you should charge $15 for it:

1/3 of your retail price covers the cost of printing the book – $5.00

1/3 covers the cost to replace the copy of the book you just sold – $5.00

1/3 is revenue or profit, to be applied to other expenses as necessary – $5.00

Don't forget to factor in shipping costs when figuring out your actual costs and, thus, your margins.

This structure has created an easy pricing method. Some of my products have higher margins (like my deluxe editions).

If you offer discounts, make sure they're designed to incentivize readers to buy more books. Don't offer a discount for no reason; make sure you get something out of it as well (aside from just the sale).

This can mean a variety of different things. For example, my omnibuses are priced lower than buying all the individuals in a series. The reader gets a deal, but in all actuality, the margins are better on my omnibuses than if they buy the individual books.

My omnibus prices are based on my multi-book prices, so if a trilogy of individual books costs $45, the omnibus will cost $40. Because I can print my omnibuses for cheaper (one book, just with more pages), I end up making more money overall, and that's the goal, right?

What's the best way for authors to maximize sales without coming across as a jerk?

When you're selling books, you have to simultaneously hold two principles in your head:

I'm here to sell books.

I'm here to connect with readers.

They may seem contradictory at first, but if you do them both correctly, they harmonize nicely with each other.

My approach is a straightforward, repeatable process that I endeavor to control from the beginning to the end. When I see someone has taken notice of my books or my display, I greet them and ask, "What kind of books do you like to read?" This question serves as an invitation to 1. connect with me and 2. take a closer look at the books I'm selling.

Once they reply, I hand them a book (connecting) that is closest to their stated interests or genre preferences, and

I begin to tell them (selling) about the books.

For each of my books and series, I've mastered my elevator pitch. Each pitch is designed to provide examples of other works comparable to my books (connecting) and also to hook and tantalize readers (selling) so they want to read the back cover of the book I'm showing them.

The back cover copy functions more or less the same as the elevator pitch, just in written form; it both connects to the reader by noting comparable titles and is written in a captivating way so as to sell them the book.

From that point on, I can either close the sale (selling) or, if they're curious about my other titles, show those off (connecting).

Don't forsake the upsell, either; if they've said "I want this one," that's your opportunity to say, "If you like this one, you'll also like this other one (connecting) because reasons... (selling)." This works for selling your entire series, it works for selling comparable titles you may also have available, and it works for selling "extras" like metal bookmarks, art prints of your characters, stickers, or whatever else you have available.

Payment details are exactly that: just details. Get paid, and focus on connection from that point on. Specifically, offer readers a chance to join your author newsletter right then and there. I always ask, "Would you like to join my newsletter?" Then I put a device in front of them, they enter their email address, and they get added to the list.

The main reasons I do this are twofold: First, adding them after they've made a purchase means they're a qualified lead. They've already invested time and money into your work, which is arguably the strongest indicator that they'll do so again. Almost everyone on my newsletter list is someone who is already a fan to some degree.

Second, I do this on the back end because doing it on the front end discourages sales, especially if you offer a free giveaway when they sign up. Why buy anything when they can try you out for free to see if you're worth their time and investment? Better to make a sale now and offer the freebie as a bonus at the end, which will further endear them to you.

Selling and connecting are two sides of the same coin. Do both at once, and you won't come across as pushy. More importantly, if you succeed at doing both, your readers will become lifelong fans, and they will continue to look for you and buy your next book(s) forever.

Chapter 9

The Art of the Blurb

As an author, you've likely spent countless hours, days, or even years meticulously weaving words into a narrative that you hope will captivate readers. However, before a reader decides to dive into the depths of your story, they'll likely encounter something far less voluminous yet equally crucial: your book's blurb. The blurb is your book's first impression, its handshake with potential readers, and its opportunity to make a compelling case for why someone should invest their time and emotions into the story you've created. In this article, we'll explore why crafting a good blurb is vital and provide tips to make yours as effective as possible.

Why Blurbs Matter

1. Attraction: A well-crafted blurb acts like a magnet. Its primary job is to attract the attention of potential readers and pull them towards choosing your book over countless others on the shelf or online store. It's a critical marketing tool that can significantly influence sales and reader engagement.

2. Information and Intrigue: A blurb should strike a delicate balance between providing enough information about the book to make it understandable and maintaining enough mystery to intrigue the reader. It sets the stage for the story without giving away crucial plot points.

3. Setting Expectations: The blurb also helps set expectations in terms of genre, tone, pace, and style. It's a litmus test for readers to know whether the book matches their interests or mood at that moment.

Tips for Crafting an Effective Blurb

1. Start Strong: The opening line of your blurb should grab the reader's attention immediately. Consider starting with a question, a provocative statement, or a powerful observation that hooks the reader.

2. Focus on Conflict and Stakes: At its core, a blurb should highlight the central conflict of the story or the main character's dilemma. This doesn't mean revealing the climax or key twists, but rather setting up the stakes and the challenges the characters face.

3. Keep it Concise and Engaging: A blurb is not a place for deep exposition. Instead, it should be a concise and snappy overview of your story that entices the reader to learn more. Aim for about 150-200 words, keeping language tight and impactful.

4. Show the Book's Spirit: Convey the tone of the book in your blurb. If your book is humorous, let some of that humor shine through. If it's a dark thriller, maintain a tense and mysterious tone in the blurb. The style and mood of the blurb should align with the style and mood of your book.

5. Use Emotional Appeal: Try to connect emotionally with the reader. Highlight characters' struggles or desires that readers might empathize with or find compelling. Emotional connection can be a powerful motivator for readers to pick up a book.

6. Avoid Clichés and Gimmicks: While it's important to catch the reader's attention, relying on overused phrases or sensational claims can turn readers off. Keep your language original and true to your story.

7. Edit Ruthlessly: Just as with your manuscript, editing is crucial. The blurb should be polished, well-crafted, and error-free. This might also mean writing several versions and testing them out with beta readers or using A/B testing in online platforms.

8. Include Critical Accolades or Comparisons, If Applicable: If your book has received accolades or can be compared to other well-known works, mentioning this in the blurb can help establish credibility and attract readers who enjoy similar books.

Crafting the perfect blurb is a blend of art and marketing strategy, requiring you to distill your complex narrative into a few compelling sentences. It's worth taking the time to perfect your blurb, as this little block of text can have a disproportionate impact on your book's success. Remember, a good blurb doesn't just summarize your book; it sells it.

The Formula for Effective Blurbs

Remember, blurbs should be a maximum of 150-200 words, so it's imperative you give potential readers enough to entice them. The formula for blurbs consist of the following:

1. The hook - a quick, immediate one or two lines to reel a reader in and make them want more.

2. Introduce your main character and their main challenge. Not a whole life summary, just the main challenge.

3. Introduce the second main character, if you have one, and how they relate to the main character and the main character's challenge.

4. Tell what's at stake. If the main character fails, who or what's lost? Does the world end? Do they die? Does someone end up ruining an important relationship?

To help you pinpoint what SHOULD be in your blurb, use these guides:

1. The one unusual or shocking takeaway from this book is _____. This will be your hook. It should not give away a surprise ending, but tease it, such as "Sometimes the only way to save the world from darkness is to find the darkness within."

2. The main character's name is _____ and their most important goal for this book is to _____. This should be personal and emotional - it's a way to get readers to invest in your main character before they even begin reading.

3. The second most important character in this book is _____. This person is connected to the main character by _. This person is connected to the main character's goal because _____.

4. If the main character doesn't achieve their goal it would be terrible for them because _____.

If you can fill these in, that's what your blurb needs to cover. Anything else is superfluous and confuses things. Once you've filled in the blanks, take your results and flesh things out, organizing it so everything makes sense.

Here's a blurb I wrote for an authors using this formula:

How do you find a victim when the witness can't remember the crime?

Ivy Preston's life takes an unforeseen turn when she witnesses a chilling kidnapping, but an accident leaves her with a problem—a concussion that erases her memory of the crime. Now, Ivy isn't just a witness, she's a blank slate in the face of danger.

As the kidnapper tightens his noose around Ivy, Detective Tomas Benson is desperate to piece together a puzzle with missing fragments. No one matching the victim's description has been reported missing, and a piece of evidence left at the crime scene has the DNA of someone who died five years ago.

In this heart-stopping crime thriller, the shadows hold the answers... but as they deepen, so does the mystery, leaving Ivy and Detective Benson teetering on the precipice of an unsolved abyss.

Will they emerge from the darkness unscathed, or will the truth remain forever lost in the shadows?

Chapter 10

Paid Newsletter Resources

General Newsletters

AuthorsXP.com

BookAngel.co.uk

BookDoggy.com

BookLoversHeaven.com

BookOfTheDay.org

BookRaid.com

BookRebel.com

ChoosyBookworm.com

eBookBetty

eBookDealsToday.com

eBookDealsToday.co.uk

eBookDiscovery.com

eBookSoda.com

EarlyBirdBooks.com (an Open Road Media company – see note below)

eReaderCafe

EreaderNewsToday

Freebooksy

GreatBooksGreatDeals.com

IndieBookLounge.com

JustKindleBooks.com

LitRing

ManyBooks.net

MyBookPlace.net

NewFreeKindleBooks.com

OneStopFiction.com

ReadCheaply.com

ReadFree.ly

ReadingDeals.com

RobinReads.com

SnicksList.com

TheFussyLibrarian.com

YourNewBooks.com

Romance Newsletters

A Love So True (an Open Road Media company – see note below)

BadBoyRomance.com

BrazenBookshelf

CraveRomance

ExciteSteam.com

FullHeartsRomance.com

HiddenGemsBooks.com

ILoveBooksAndStuff

LoveKissedBooks

PillowTalkBooks.com

Pretty-Hot.com

RedRosesRomance.com

Romance.io

ShamelessBookDeals.com

TheSweetestRomance

ToplessCowboy

Unearthly Ever Afters

Wolf Pack Co-op

Mystery / thriller / horror Newsletters

BookAdrenaline.com

Murder & Mayhem (an Open Road Media company – see note below)

Patty's Ebookaroo

The Lineup (an Open Road Media company – see note below)

Sci-Fi / Fantasy Newsletters

BookBarbarian

Geektastic

Patty's Ebookaroo

The Portalist (an Open Road Media company – see note below)

History / Historical Newsletters

The Archive (an Open Road Media company – see note below)

Christian Newsletters

Faithful Reads

1531 Entertainment

Foreign Language Newsletters

eBookNinja.de

*Open Road Media: This is a group of newsletters, each with their own branding and focus. They don't actually have a submission form on their site; their submission form is here: https://openroad.typeform.com/to/iqqvqa

About the author

Richard Fierce is a dynamic voice in the realms of fantasy and space opera, weaving tales that transport readers to worlds beyond imagination. His journey as a wordsmith began in childhood, but it was in 2007 that he took the plunge into the world of publishing. Since then, Richard has enchanted readers with multiple novels and short stories, showcasing his versatility and creativity.

In the year 2000, Richard Fierce earned the esteemed title of Poet of the Year for his captivating poem, "The Darkness." This early recognition hinted at the depth and artistry that would define his future literary endeavors.

Beyond the written word, Richard is a co-founder of the Acworth Book Festival, a significant literary event held in Acworth, Georgia. This initiative reflects his commitment to fostering a vibrant literary community and celebrating the written word.

A resilient spirit, Richard transitioned from a career in retail to the dynamic tech industry, finding new inspiration and challenges in the world of technology when he's not immersed in crafting fantastical tales.

In his personal life, Richard is a family man, navigating the joys and challenges of marriage and parenting. With three step-daughters (pray for him), three grandchildren, a menagerie of four dogs (his beloved huskies!), and two ferrets, his home is a lively haven that resembles a bustling zoo.

Richard's enduring love for fantasy was sparked in high school when a friend's mother gifted him a copy of "Dragons of Spring Dawning" by Margaret Weis and Tracy Hickman. This transformative experience ignited a passion that has since shaped his literary career, inspiring him to create worlds where dragons soar, and adventures unfold.

You can find his other books and more information at his website at www.richardfierce.com